The Serene Home

Decorating Secrets
& Inspirations

The Serene Home

Decorating Secrets
& Inspirations

Eileen Cannon Paulin

Sterling Publishing Co., Inc. New York

A Sterling/Chapelle Book

Chapelle, Ltd.

Owner: Jo Packham

By: Eileen Cannon Paulin

Photographed by: Wanelle Fitch

Produced and Styled by: Eileen Cannon Paulin

Graphic Design by: LaMar Norman

Library of Congress
Cataloging-in-Publication Data

Paulin, Eileen Cannon.
  The serene home : decorating secrets &
inspirations / Eileen Cannon Paulin.
        p. cm.
"A Sterling/Chapelle Book."
  Includes index.
  ISBN 1-40270-403-8
  1.   Interior decoration--Psychological aspects.
      I. Title.
NK2113 .P38 2003
747--dc21

                              2002151919

10 9 8 7 6 5 4 3 2 1

Published by Sterling Publishing Co. Inc.
387 Park Avenue South, New York, N.Y. 10016
©2003 by Eileen Cannon Paulin
Distributed in Canada by Sterling Publishing
⅟ Canadian Manda Group, One Atlantic Avenue, Suite 105
Toronto, Ontario, Canada M6K 3E7
Distributed in Great Britain by Chrysalis Books
64 Brewery Road, London N7 9NT, England
Distributed in Australia by Capricorn Link (Australia) Pty. Ltd.
P. O. Box 704, Windsor, NSW 2756, Australia
Printed and Bound in China

Sterling ISBN 1-4027-0403-8

Every effort has been made to ensure
that all of the information in the book is
accurate.

If you have any questions or comments,
please contact:

Chapelle, Ltd., Inc.
P. O. Box 9252
Ogden, UT 84409
e-mail: chapelle@chapelleltd.com
web site: www.chapelleltd.com

The Photographer

As with all good things in life, *The Serene Home* was a team effort. Photographer Wanelle Fitch recorded all the images you see in this book. We stood side-by-side, many times laughing till we cried, and without her commitment this book never would have been created.

Wanelle Fitch is an extremely versatile photographer whose genres include portraiture, fashion, advertising, fine art and interiors. Her celebrity portraits include Gene Wilder, Christine McVie and Deepak Chopra. A partial list of her clientele includes Helen Kaminski, Vogue and Cartier. Wanelle holds a Master of Fine Arts from Art Center College of Design and a Bachelor of Arts from the University of Southern California.

The Author

Eileen Cannon Paulin has had a lifelong passion for writing and decorating. Happiest when finding and sharing other people's stories, she delights in her work as editor of *Romantic Homes* Magazine, and as a regular guest on home decorating shows including; The Christopher Lowell Show on The Discovery Channel, and You're Home: With Kitty Bartholomew, Smart Solutions and other decorating shows on HGTV. She is also associate publisher of *Victorian Homes* Magazine.

Eileen is a journalism graduate of The University of Southern California and has over 23 years experience in magazine publishing. She lives in Southern California with her husband and two children. Her home is an ever-changing scene of countless home decorating and makeover projects.

In Tribute:

To my husband Stephen and children Brendan and Sarah, for their support and patience while I pursue my love of writing and decorating. To my father David, the legacy of my mother Mary Ellen, and my dear friends, for always believing in me. To the "Homes Girls," for their unwavering support.

Thank You

The seven home owners who opened their homes to us were welcoming and kind. Our days photographing their homes are wonderful memories. Thank you to Judy Watkins for her undying support, and help in our visits to the Central Coast of California. You know the true meaning of the word friend.

Table of Contents

10

34

58

A small tract home is transformed into a quiet sanctuary and given character with old moldings, painted wood floors, and tranquil areas for reading, writing and working.

Life in this artist's cottage is like being on retreat everyday. Ideas for creative vignettes, mantle displays and outdoor living abound, as well as tips on creating cottage style.

With a quick turn of pillows and cushions, and removal of a few slipcovers, you can have a look that changes with the seasons. Whether you sew yourself, or use a professional, these ideas will inspire you to try a change.

Displaying collectibles and treasures without a cluttered look is one of the secrets in this small loft.

Introduction

Serenity is a very personal state of mind, and can only be found deep down inside. However, our environment greatly influences our psyche, which is why the manner in which we organize and decorate our home is an important part of our well-being.

There is a very simple formula for creating a serene home. It has to make *you* feel good. A home that fits your personal style is the right home for you. It should make your heart sing and bring you happiness in the time you spend there. Creating such a home is often a journey. As we evolve, so do our priorities and preferences.

For some, serenity is an all-white house with very little in it; for another, serenity is living amidst dozens of collections and countless pieces of antique furniture. What most serene homes have in common is that they are decorated for comfort, and clearly reflect the interests and passions of the people who live there.

By nature, we are all a bit nosy about how other people live. Books, magazines and television shows make it possible for us to get inside other people's homes and take a peek. We take away ideas we can customize and use in our own homes. It's my hope that this book will help make your own home a source of comfort and joy.

Seven gracious home owners have opened their doors and allowed us to come inside and share their decorating ideas. Each of these homes is distinctly different, but in their own way, they are all peaceful and tranquil. Enjoy!

Eileen Cannon Paulin

"When we sip tea, we are on our way to serenity."
—*Alexandra Stoddard*

"Go confidently in the direction of your dreams. Live the life you have imagined."
— *Henry David Thoreau*

An antique mirror, telephone and art print, along with a reproduction urn, make a charming vignette reminiscent of days gone by.

The Friendly Farmhouse

Set in the pastoral countryside, Gary and Nancy Bagnall's restored farmhouse is home to an active family of four and a menagerie of pets. The original rooms of the house date back to the 1800s, and inspire a relaxed vintage decorating style that handles the wear and tear of everyday life. Intimate seating areas throughout the house invite quiet moments, and small decorative vignettes showcase Gary's passion for collecting antique aquariums and accessories.

(Left) The wraparound porch with decorative millwork, and the fish-scale shingles are a testimony to the farmhouse's Victorian roots.

The bright and inviting living room owes its cheerfulness to the soft yellow walls and large windows. Vintage lace panels hung from café rods add elegance to the room, and provide just enough privacy without blocking light.

Serene Secret

Vintage tablecloths can be easily sewn to create soft window coverings. Sew a pocket along the top of the panel and insert a curtain rod.

A formal Victorian love seat and cherry coffee table mixes with an overstuffed sofa and softly worn antique cabinet to make the living room elegant and casual at the same time. It's welcoming to guests, but not intimidating for everyday use.

> "Order is a lovely thing; on disarray it lays
> its wing, teaching simplicity to sing."
> —Anna Branch

Serene Secrets

Vintage napkins have many uses far and beyond their original intent. They are a lovely way to soften furniture displays in all types of cabinets and shelves.

Vintage linens abound at flea markets and antiques stores, but are often stained and yellowed. "The care of beautiful antique linens is a labor of love," says linen expert Paula Gins. Her tried-and-true method for reviving and maintaining vintage linens is reliable and easy.

Use your washing machine on the gentle cycle with cold water. For a small load, add ½ scoop of powdered detergent, ⅛ cup of bluing and 1 scoop of non-chlorinated bleach. Agitate machine to dissolve all powders before adding linens. In the last deep-water rinse, add ½ cup white vinegar to remove detergent residue.

Dry linens, using the dryer's gentle setting, or hang outside to line-dry. When ironing, do not dampen linen. Use a dry iron on the middle setting. Pad the ironing board with several cotton Turkish towels. Iron on the wrong side, and use spray starch.

Stubborn stains should be soaked in a combination of powdered detergent and powdered non-chlorinated bleach in a glass bowl. Tough stains can be treated by heating the same mixture in a porcelain pot and simmering the linens for 10–20 minutes.

To maintain uniform color for matching linens, such as napkins, be sure to wash them all together each time you launder.

(Right) The peeling paint on a vintage cabinet is a delightful feature. The simple arrangements are a tranquil addition to the room.

The master bedroom should be the most serene room in the house. It's here that you begin and conclude each day. More than any room, the décor of the bedroom should appeal to your innermost preferences. Cater to and soothe yourself by painting this room your favorite color.

(Above) The fireplace mantel in the master bedroom is kept simple. Layering a small piece of art over a large antique mirror provides depth. The pieces on either end of the mantel are from the home owner's collection of antique aquariums.

(Left) Small vignettes that reflect your special interests and include favorite possessions are a delight to put together. If arranged from the heart, a small display will bring you joy every time you pass by.

The bedroom is kept simple by using all-white furniture. The subtle green walls are calming and accessories are kept to a minimum. Angling a small armoire in the corner softens the sharp angles of the room, and makes the sitting area more intimate.

"There is no need to go to India or anywhere else to find peace. You will find that deep place of silence right in your room, your garden or even your bathtub."
—*Elisabeth Kubler-Ross*

This all-white bathroom is a classically serene sanctuary. The use of beadboard preserves the vintage character of the house. Flea market finds, such as the metal shelf on the wall, an old bureau and the vanity stool marry well with the modern conveniences of a jetted tub and tile shower to create a casually elegant retreat.

The crackle finish on the bureau sink cabinet is easy to achieve with a two-step finish kit sold at craft stores.

19

"Home, the spot of earth supremely blest,
a dearer, sweeter spot than all the rest."
—*Robert Montgomery*

The bathroom sink cabinet becomes a focal point because of its elegance and muted color. Dropping a modern sink into an antique cabinet has become a popular way to add ambiance to a bathroom.

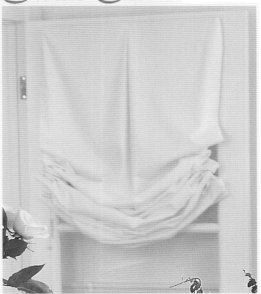

Glass interior doors allow light to pass from room to room. A Roman or balloon shade can provide privacy when needed, and adds a soft designer touch.

Bringing collections out from inside cabinets and closets is one of the easiest ways to bring comfort and joy to your décor. Collections generally take form because of a love of something, and you may have a collection without realizing it. Perhaps you have numerous bottles and vases around the house that are all cut glass. Gather together things with common materials or colors for interesting displays.

(Above) A small vignette of vintage perfume bottles and toiletry containers is simple and adds elegance to the bathroom. Set on a wall shelf, the display adds ambiance without taking up counter space.

(Left) The ultimate serenity comes from nature. Here a collection of birds' nests and eggs create a simple grouping that evokes peace and harmony with the outdoors. Be sure birds' nests are abandoned before removing them, and be thoughtful by using faux eggs for decorative displays.

Once relegated to display shelves, these antique aquarium figurines bring a whimsical touch to the master bath.

Light green painted cabinets and walls, combined with subtle rose-colored tile, make the kitchen soft and peaceful despite the constant activity that takes place in it. The muted colors are a welcome alternative to the all-white kitchens often seen in remodeled farmhouses. Pewter bin pulls on the drawers, and the farmhouse sink provide a tribute to the house's origins.

Decorative vignettes in the kitchen can be practical too. Cooking herbs are easily at hand when incorporated into displays, and the beauty of a special cake is celebrated by putting it in a place of honor.

Serene Secret

An oval mirror makes a wonderful tray for displaying collectibles and enhancing vignettes. A mirror with an ornate frame adds architectural texture and character to a room.

Serene Secret

Small lamps bring warm lighting into a kitchen. Once the work is done and it's time to enjoy a meal, bright overhead lights can be turned off and the lamp will gracefully illuminate the kitchen.

(Above) The red motifs of transferware add a touch of color to a soft room.

(Right) This trio of antique aquariums is put to use for displays on the kitchen shelf. The contents are changed with the seasons, and include glass ornaments for the winter holidays and eggs for springtime.

Ornate Additions

Wood embellishments can be easily added to furniture for a rich decorative touch. Available through mail-order sources or at many home improvement stores, wood appliqués may be painted or stained and attached to furniture using carpenter's glue.

Bowled Over

Antique aquariums are rare and expensive. Affordable reproductions can be used for decoration or put to practical use holding staples like sugar and flour.

The Friendly Farmhouse

Soft Shower

An antique lace bedcover hides the shower and softens the bathroom. Use a large tablecloth for the same look. Metal rings help the covering slide easily out of the way when the shower is in use.

Daytime Romance

Candles don't need to be relegated to nighttime. They are perfect around the tub for a bath—anytime of day or night. Using an array of sizes, and as many as you wish, creates instant serenity.

Faux—You Know!

This sink cabinet has an elegant and expensive look. Closer inspection shows a secret that saves cost—the counter is a marbleized paint finish on wood—not the real thing. Achieve the same look with a faux-finish kit.

Create Your Own

While the look of multiple mirrors hung on walls has become popular, the cost of these little gems has risen at flea markets and consignment shops. With a little scouting around, you can create the same look.

Look for frames with character. Try not to be distracted by the color—it can always be changed with a coat of paint.

Be on the lookout for various shapes and sizes of frames. The more you vary the shapes, the more interesting your wall arrangement will be.

Shop for ornate embellishment pieces at home improvement stores or on-line.

Attach the decorative piece to the top of the mirror, using either carpenter's glue or a welding gel compound. Clamp the piece in place while the adhesive dries.

Vintage-Style Mirror

Mask the mirror with painter's tape, and spray-paint the frame.

Once the paint is dry, you can either leave it alone, or apply a fresh coat.

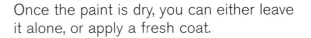

If you prefer a gilded finish, it can easily be added with a rub-on metallic wax.

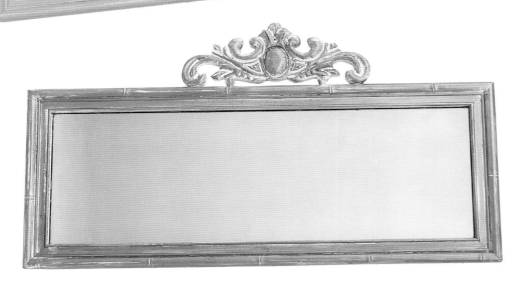

"An Englishman's home is his castle."
—*Proverb*

John built the potting shed as a Mother's Day gift for Kim. Located in the side yard, it's close to the house so Kim can sneak out for quiet moments, preparing plants for the gardening she dearly loves.

A Mountainton Manor

Approaching the home of John and Kim Stanier evokes classic fairy tales of kings and queens in far-off lands. Set on a hilltop overlooking eighty-five acres, the outside of the castle-like home is stately and charming. The first indication that the inside is actually very casual, warm, and welcoming is a sign by the front door that tells visitors to "Wipe Your Bloody Feet!" John, an Englishman by birth, commutes all over the world as a successful cinematographer. Kim, an interior designer, has created a tranquil home that graciously handles the active antics of three young children and a menagerie of pets.

This dream house is well lived-in and filled with serene decorating ideas that can be translated into any home.

(Left) The best perspective of the Stanier's house is high on a hill above the trees, looking down from the children's fort.

The dining room is kept simple, and ready to greet guests at a moment's notice. The ladder-back chairs are casual, while a collection of antique mirrors arranged on the wall provides elegant formality.

"The ornament of a house is the friends who frequent it."
—*Ralph Waldo Emerson*

Serene Secret

Layer different sizes of tablecloths to soften a large dining table. Mix colors and patterns for a designer touch. Change the mix of linens to suit the season.

"There is nothing like staying
at home for real comfort."
—Jane Austen

Create simple and serene ambiance by
grouping objects of the same color and tones
together. Antique and new silver pieces may
differ in their design, but the common color
ties the grouping together.

Window seats invite quiet times of
reflection, and are the perfect place for
writing or reading. This seat runs the full
width of the window, and assures that the
dining room is used regularly—not just
when entertaining company. Pillows of
varying shapes make it easy for any size
person to get into a comfortable position.

(Right) The buffet and a large oil painting bring stately European sophistication
to the otherwise relaxed dining room.

38

A vignette on an ottoman can be easily moved when it is called into duty as a table or footrest. Trays provide a flat surface for displays and make it easy to move decorative accessories.

Serene Secret

Small vignettes—much like still life paintings—warm a home. Often, they tell a story of the people that live there. For the most inviting groupings, vary the height of objects. Collections of books make good risers. When using similar items, such as candlestick holders, use the designer's Rule of Three: odd numbers of objects.

(Right) The living room is set apart from other rooms by its deep-red painted walls. The stone fireplace and a mix of antiques gathered from travels, make this formal area a haven for adult conversation and visiting.

Creating places for quiet reflection and reading is one of the most important components of a serene home. Whether you have a library, or can just set aside a small corner, comfortable seating and good lighting are the basics.

"The love of learning, the sequestered nooks, and all the sweet serenity of books."
—*Henry Wadsworth Longfellow*

In addition to books, the shelves in the library are filled with a collection of antique cameras that reflect John's passion as a cinematographer.

Serene Secret

Architectural accents can be easily added to a ceiling. Create a grid using small linear molding, then add a medallion in the center of each square. These embellishments are available at home improvement stores or through restoration company mail-order catalogs. Medallions made of resin are inexpensive and easy to affix to ceilings or walls.

"Reading
is a basic
tool in
the living
of the
good life."
—*Mortimer
Adler*

The library is stately
because of the mold-
ings, built-in book-
cases and ceiling.
The room is bright
and airy, making
it very inviting.
Placing the chair
on an angle softens
the room.

43

The cheerful family room flows naturally into the everyday eating area. Painted walls are easily wiped off or touched up. Active families are apt to nick and mark wallpaper.

Oversized furniture works well for families with young children. Slipcovers make it easy to recover from spills and dirt. The window coverings are panels of French fabric held open during the day by iron tiebacks.

Providing children with plenty of space to store toys and games can keep clutter to a minimum. A large armoire or cupboard devoted to this use makes cleanup simple and keeps everything accessible.

Angle furniture around a fireplace or entertainment center rather than lining it up to the walls. Keeping the television and stereo equipment hidden away in cabinets helps keep a room soft.

A small chair makes a child feel at home and provides the perfect spot for a beloved small pet.

• Filling a box with postcards from family and friend's travels makes a wonderful conversation piece and a nice display for a coffee table.

• Decorating a box for postcards is a fun project. Purchase an unfinished wood box at a craft store. Paint it a color that matches your décor, and line the inside with an old map. Affix a favorite card to the lid.

Colors and patterns mix comfortably if you stay within the same color palette. The pillows on this window seat add warmth and a touch of whimsy to the room. Stripes, polka dots and toile work well together and invite the passerby to curl up and rest awhile.

An additional seating area at one end of the family room is away from the television room, which makes a quiet place for conversation and reading. The high-back chair on the left is a twin to one in the living room. They can be put together in either room for additional seating.

"The foolish man
seeks happiness in
the distance, the
wise man grows it
under his feet."
—*Proverb*

Serene Secret

Distressed or aged furniture
finishes are a great choice for
tables and chairs in a family
eating area. They handle wear
and tear with ease, making family
meals worry free.

Family meals are served at the farmhouse table in this sunny room adjacent
to the main living area. The children
each have their own chair, while the
adults use the bench.

The day's comings and goings are coordinated in the kitchen. The use of white with blue accents creates a calm room. Glass interior doors allow light into adjacent rooms, but can be closed to keep the noise of meal preparation from the rest of the house.

"No matter where I serve my guests, They always like my kitchen best."
—*Unknown*

A tile backsplash behind the stove extends to the top of the cabinets, and makes cleanup easy. Tile backsplashes run above all the countertop areas and help keep kitchen maintenance to a minimum.

Serene Secret

Give your kitchen a custom look by adding turned furniture legs to the corners of cabinets. You can also enlarge or extend the size of an island countertop and use the legs at the overhanging end. Turned furniture legs can be purchased at home improvement stores.

Good lighting is an essential element for a serene kitchen. The combination of large windows and strategically placed lighting makes it easy to see and work in this kitchen. Consider putting windows over work areas so that natural light is optimized when preparing food and doing kitchen chores. A large light fixture hung over the island illuminates the area at night, and wall sconces over the sink provide soft mood lighting. Also consider installing lighting under cabinets to light countertop work areas.

A simple garden design creates an outside dining room that is a peaceful setting for family meals and conversations. Use natural elements to define intimate outdoor spaces. Kim created the feeling of a room in the garden by first laying a low stone wall in front of a row of mature trees. Rosebushes serve as one wall of the area, while a combination of fast growing shrubs and geraniums complete the third partition. The front of the outdoor room faces the house, and is graced with a garden arch covered with a flowering vine. Weather treated wood furniture stays out all year round.

Often a simple design is the most elegant. The rectangular pool reflects the simple lines of the cabana. This area is a wonderful example of the peaceful feeling balance creates. The two tall trees frame the pool, and the two potted palms, in turn, frame the cabana door. Pool furniture and accessories are kept to a minimum, and the result is a picturesque and classic area.

Charming Children's Chairs

Children's chairs bring a warm touch to any room. If you didn't inherit a chair or two, give a new chair quick history by slightly distressing it or adding a coat of paint. Make a cushion to match your décor.

Peace of Mind

Chair seats can be easily unscrewed from the underside, and a sheet of clear plastic placed over fabric to protect it from spills. You'll continue to enjoy the fabric's color and beauty without worrying about damage.

A Mountaintop Manor

The Young Masters

Among a mother's favorite art is that of her children—and its value grows as they do. Don't relegate their masterworks to a box in the attic. Kim Stanier frames her children's art and hangs it in a hallway gallery. The frames are standard sizes that come with matting and are purchased at a frame retailer.

Stately Reflections

The frames of antique mirrors add genteel elegance to a room. An arrangement of mirrors brightens and adds wonderful play of light. Newer frames can be given a vintage feel with gold leaf rub-on wax.

57

"If you surrender completely to the moments as they pass, you will live more richly those moments."
—*Anne Morrow Lindbergh*

A coat of arms over the front door declares that Fraser House is devoted to historical and traditional style.

A Stately Grand Dame

When you start up the front walk of Fraser House, you are transported from its West Coast neighborhood to the grace and beauty of the Old South. Every detail of the house is rooted in history, making it nearly impossible to believe it is just a few years old.

Designer Ann Fraser's attention to detail and comfort have added instant ambiance and a timeworn patina to her home. Working with confidence and courage, Ann has made every room grand, while warm and welcoming at the same time.

Her home is a treasure trove of ideas that may be used to customize and add character to any style of house.

(Left) Fraser House, as designer Ann Fraser has dubbed her classic home, is reminiscent of a southern mansion with its large sweeping porches and shuttered windows. A pair of architectural pilasters with antique urns is the first hint of what lies behind the gates to this quiet and gracious beauty.

The living room extends along the entire front of the house and is divided into several conversation areas. The expansive space is brought together with soft muted tones and beautifully hand-painted walls.

Serene Secret

Pull chairs into a room and away from walls to create an intimate feeling that invites guests to, "Come and sit a spell."

The large front room of the house has three separate functions; a formal living room, a more casual sitting area with a fireplace, and an entry. A large crystal chandelier and round table in front of the door establish the center of the room as the entry hall and greeting area. The iron stair rail is sophisticated and is a dramatic alternative to wood.

Serene Secret

While hand-painted walls may seem intimidating, they are not difficult to do yourself. Learn-to-paint systems available at craft stores are designed for painting flowers, leaves and vines. If you are not inclined to try free-hand motifs, there are countless stencil patterns available.

Once the walls are finished and have cured, be sure to use a clear waterproof coat to protect your work.

(Above) Seashells are nature's reminder of the peaceful allure of the ocean and lend quiet harmony to a home.

(Right) A row of small antique books and a select number of treasures on a desktop create an inviting place for moments of quiet writing or reading.

"Behind every man's busy-ness there should be a level of undisturbed serenity."
—*Henry David Thoreau*

Set aside a spot for solitude when planning seating areas in your home. Add a footstool and a small side table for comfort. If possible, create this special place where there is plenty of natural light during the day.

Small tabletops become still life works of art when used to display an eclectic blend of collectibles. The most enjoyable thing about this part of decorating is that there are no rules. A small tabletop is the perfect place to showcase antique books and small works of art. When arranging displays next to a seating area, sit down and create the arrangement from the eye level of the person seated in the chair. Be sure to vary heights and textures.

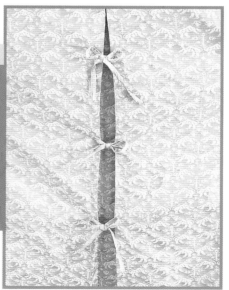

Serene Secret

Slipcovered chairs—like an elegant woman's evening gown—can have a surprise in the back. An inverted pleat, held together with three small bows, gives a chair a special touch.

The fireplace is the focal point of this seating area where slipcovered chairs are mixed with a Victorian fainting couch.

• Today's sewing machines make it possible to create large monograms at home. Custom lettering and fonts can be easily downloaded from the internet and embroidered on most fabrics.
• High-quality rayon fabrics are durable and are a good substitute for silk.

(Right) The dining chairs are monogrammed and upholstered in silk. Using a settee on one side is a nice alternative to placing chairs around the whole table.

(Left) Arched doorways become alluring when fitted with puddled tie-back drapes.

(Below) Textured or embellished fabrics bring depth and richness to a serene home.

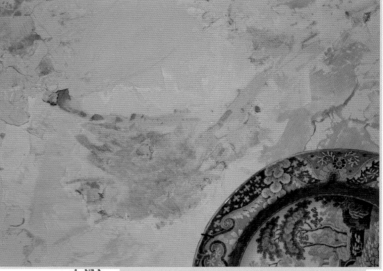

Walls can be given an Old World feel with a plaster treatment that adds instant age and dimension to a room. This stucco-like treatment is achieved using wall plaster that has been tinted pink and gray. Here several hues of pink were used before adding gray for a marbling effect. White wall plaster can be tinted with wall paint in any color you prefer, and applied with a trowel. Mix different batches of plaster for each tone you want to use. Start with the lightest color first and apply that over the entire wall surface. Follow with the other colors and blend the areas as you prefer while the plaster is still wet.

Be certain that walls are clean and sanded before starting. The plaster can set quickly, so you may prefer to work in sections.

A grand candelabrum is a romantic light source for evening
dinners and crowns a symmetrical display atop a small buffet.

Riding boots and the collection on the desk in the sitting room suggest the travels of a worldly country gentleman. Accessories that reflect your interests and tell a story make interesting vignettes.

The arrangement on the desktop has a British Colonial theme and is in keeping with the masculine undertones of the sitting room.

Serene Secret

Two walls in the sitting room are covered with stone and mortar. This treatment gives the room the hard-hewn feel of an historic country estate. This wall treatment can be tricky to do yourself, and is probably best done by a stone mason.

A basket filled with shells is a lovely accent to a room, and is a wonderful way to enjoy memories of relaxing days spent hunting and gathering along the shore.

73

A classic oil portrait looks down over the sitting room and its eclectic furnishings. The picture suggests that generations of family have inhabited the house—which in reality was just recently built.

"The butterfly counts not months but moments, and has enough time."
—*Rabindranath Tagore*

Counter stools in the kitchen are covered with tapestry-print cotton fabric. On the back of the stools, the fabric is folded and secured with a piece of vintage jewelry.

A corner of the kitchen is reserved for an elegant vignette counterbalanced by whimsical Chinese lanterns.

A stately canopy bed is sumptuous when dressed with silk curtains and layered bedding.

The texture on the walls in the master bedroom was achieved by painting over wallpaper with metallic silver paint. It may be necessary to use a primer coat over the wallpaper before applying the metallic paint. Experiment with a sample before you go to work on wallpaper that is already hung.

(Above) Architectural salvage pieces such as a large bookcase give a room historical elegance.

(Right) Monograms make a home your own. Ann Fraser purchased these lace-inset silk curtains in Paris, and counts them among her favorite treasures.

(Above) Starfish arranged over a doorway blend quietly with the wall covering, and celebrate gifts from the sea. The starfish are hung on small finishing nails.

(Left) The master bathroom includes a large dressing area. Sunlit daytime soaks in the tub are possible because the tub is centered in front of large windows.

"One cannot collect all the beautiful shells on the beach
One can collect only a few, and they are more beautiful if they are few."

—*Anne Morrow Lindbergh*

A whimsical portrait makes sure things in this exquisite bathroom aren't taken too seriously. Monogrammed towels are mixed with souvenirs from stays at a favorite Paris hotel.

Serene Secret

Fabric-covered walls contribute to a room's richness, help soften sounds and make a room serene.

Comforts & Joys from
A Stately Grand Dame

Calm and Cool Blue

Blue-and-white china and pottery mix well with any decorating color palette. Import stores carry many inexpensive choices.

Dutch Treat

A Dutch door is a wonderful way to let in light and fresh air while promoting informality that invites neighbors to come in for a visit.

Please Be Seated

Treat outdoor seating areas as you would any other room, and you will create an elegant and comfortable outdoor space. The hanging light fixture, statuary and accessories pull this seating space together and make it a gracious extension to the house.

She Saves Seashells

Flowerpots can be easily covered with shells. Glue shells to the pot with permanent cement, then fill in crevices and spaces with tile grout.

Draped Doorways

(Above) While the Victorians draped doorways to retain heat in certain rooms, you can bring elegance and soften sounds by sewing drapes for interior doorways. Puddling expensive fabric on the floor was once a sign of wealth, and still adds richness to a room.

Stamps of Approval

(Right) Expensive fabrics need not be out of reach. You can stamp or emboss your own velvet before sewing the fabric into curtains. Craft stores sell kits for stamping fabric. For a special touch, use metallic fabric paint.

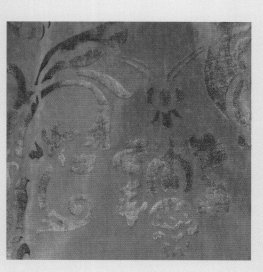

An Easy-to-Make Serene

The powder room of Fraser House is a symphony of seashells, and the focal point is an exquisite seashell-framed mirror. This large mirror frame works well in this stately home.

This small seashell mirror is an antique. It shows ideas for arranging shells for a symmetrical look.

84

Seashell Mirror

Making a seashell-framed mirror for your own home is a simple and fun project. Use a variety of shells you have collected, or purchase matching shells for a more uniform look.

Be certain that the shells are clean and dry. It is a good idea to soak shells in warm water and bleach to remove dirt and odors before you begin the project.

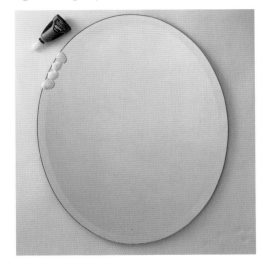

Begin with a piece of mirror in any shape. This round beveled-edge mirror was purchased at a large retail store for less than twenty dollars.

Arrange clean shells in any pattern you choose. Use quick-dry permanent glue to adhere the shells to the edge of the mirror. Any excess glue on the mirror can be removed later with a razor blade.

Add as many shells as you prefer, this particular mirror is kept simple with a single row of all-white shells. Allow the glue to dry for several hours before hanging the mirror.

"First keep the peace within your-self, then you can also bring peace to others."
—*Thomas Kempsis*

Treasures from frequent buying trips inevitably find their way home, where they are carefully placed into simple still life displays such as this one in the entry hall.

A Bungalow by the Beach

Most often, serenity is a choice. It's gained by making a conscious decision to be happy in the present with what we have. Judy Watkins has chosen serenity and created a home that helps her to maintain a joyful balanced family and business. Her beachside bungalow is a soft assembly of cherished possessions with special spaces for reading, writing, working and meditating.

Her home and her business—like the mirrors she loves to decorate with—are a reflection of her passions and the choice that she has made to keep her life simply serene.

(Left) The doors along the back wall of the living room open into the backyard. Vintage lace panels and salvaged pieces, like the screen door, make their way around the house as the décor continually changes to suit the seasons and new acquisitions.

The soft tones of the wooden floors and painted walls are an harmonic backdrop for the open living room. Large doors and windows allow natural light to bathe the room.

The biggest challenge in decorating a tract house is figuring out how to give it character. The true decorating genius can do it without spending a large amount of money. Architectural antiques are one of the easiest fixes. The trick is to look beyond the obvious. A corner cupboard can make a boring corner an interesting place for displaying collections. An old door or shutters can be used to mask aluminum doors and windows.

(Above) Using a large fireplace surround would have been off-scale for this room. Instead, just the antique mantel was used, which creates a focal point for the room. The oval mirror reflects artwork and mirrors on the opposite wall.

(Left) Placing a lamp on a table behind a large comfortable chair—rather than next to it—puts the light source in a better location and makes it easier to read in the evenings.

The neutral tones throughout the house make it easy to move accessories around. Here, an antique enamelware coffeepot complements red transferware dishes and provides some bright color.

(Left) Two sizes of old painted shutters, and a lace panel tied in the center, soften the window over the eating area. This treatment masks the metal window frames and softly filters the light.

(Right) A small open shelf over the built-in desk in the kitchen showcases white pitchers. Displaying family photos under glass allows them to be enjoyed without the clutter of numerous small frames.

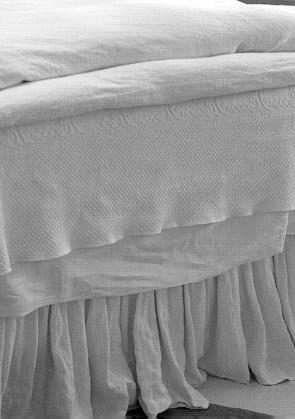

Painted white wooden floors reflect light and help create a soft glow in a room. Light scuffing and wear add to the relaxed look. They can be lightly sanded and repainted every few years. Special paint formulated for floors works best and is worth the investment.

(Left) The color palette in the master bedroom is soft and tranquil. Layers of vintage white linen and feather duvets make the bed soft and appealing. The rug adds color while its round shape softens the room.

(Below) The top of a bedside table is covered with linen and arranged with favorite old books and a small angel. The custom lamp shade, made from vintage fabric, makes the alabaster lamp a showpiece.

(Left) Green walls make the home office a cheerful place to work. By keeping work clutter to a minimum and out of sight, the room is peaceful and feels like a retreat instead of a constant reminder of tasks waiting to be completed.

(Right) Decorative vignettes warm the room, but don't take up valuable work-space. The top of the armoire holds an eclectic collection with one thing in common—everything is white.

(Above) A wooden trug keeps stationery and pencils organized. A glass flower frog is tucked into a compartment and holds sharpened pencils.

(Right) While the bathroom is small, it makes up in charm what it lacks in space. New white tile and plumbing fixtures mix well with an antique mirror and a salvaged window hung from the ceiling. The existing electrical fixture was painted, and beaded lightbulb covers were added.

Taking a negative and turning it into a positive often achieves serenity. Blemished wood can be painted. Blank walls can be given character by hanging a dimensional shelf. Mirrors can reflect light in a dark room.

(Above) What would have otherwise been a large bland wall becomes a gallery next to an antique bamboo daybed. Centering the shelf over the bed and using it for display suggests the warmth of a fireplace mantel. A grouping of reproduction clocks adds whimsy to the room.

(Left) Take time to appreciate objects for their beauty, not just their function. By putting this antique fireplace set up on a dresser, it can be admired. The wire flower frogs can be used to hold notes and reminders.

A small pillow sewn from dish towels complements a lamp shade made from vintage monogrammed linen. Keeping the walls and furniture light makes it possible to mix colors and patterns in the bedding and still maintain a serene feel.

A cozy built-in sitting bench along a wall can take the place of a chair and save valuable floor space in a small room. Placing a bed on an angle in a bedroom may take better advantage of light.

Keeping high-tech out of the bedroom is a serene choice, and a vintage telephone is a delightful touch. While there are reproductions available, an old phone can often be rewired.

"Every woman needs a writing desk."
—*Mary Ellen Cannon*

A writing desk, set aside from other work areas, is a necessity in maintaining a serene balance in your life. It should be a place for friendly correspondence. Try to relegate computers and filing systems elsewhere and maintain the sanctity of this space. Social stationery, greeting cards, favorite pens and pencils along with a few of your favorite things will make this a pleasurable spot.

(Left) A small desk can be just as wonderful as a large one. If possible, place the desk by a window for better lighting. Pretty ribbon can be used to tie notes or to organize favorite letters.

(Above) The simplest things often bring the most joy. A collection of vintage buttons adds a sweet touch and a little inspiration to this writing desk.

Soft colored walls are ideal for a serene feel, but it isn't always possible to paint all-white walls. Decorative ribbons and vintage chains can be used to hang a variety of pictures, mirrors and other collectibles to break up the expanse of white.

A collection of antique brushes and a hand mirror make a charming display on a stool at the foot of the bed.

Layering the décor of the windows, walls and bed softens this room and makes it cozy, despite the many things in it. Tie-top curtain panels cover the windows, and a young girl's sheer dress adds an interesting dimension. Ballet shoes hung from the corner of a mirror are a sweet touch.

Comforts and Joys from

Up Off the Floor

Small chairs make wonderful risers for creating height in displays. This child's chair at right is at home in the middle of the dining table.

Best Under Glass

Glass cake or cheese plate covers make an elegant substitute for a garden cloche. Placed over a vintage round mirror, anything displayed inside becomes a treasure.

A Bungalow by the Beach

Soft Slips

Much attention has been given to slipcovering furniture, but a soft slipcover is a fast and easy way to customize a lamp shade.

Under Wraps

A boring loft railing or banister can be hidden and made a focal point by layering quilts and other vintage bedding. This collection of French quilts hangs over a low wall into an open stairwell.

Simply Elegant

Interesting objects grouped together can bring elegance and style into a simple tract house. Using symmetry and balance when organizing a vignette makes it simple and prevents it from looking overdone.

Island Beauty

If a kitchen does not have an island workspace, an oval table can be centered in the middle of the room. A vignette set on an oval mirror complements the shape of the table and warms the room.

Tiny Tables

A small footstool topped with a piece of marble becomes a low table and is a delightful place to display treasures like vintage lacework and jewelry.

Basic Baskets

Antique French laundry baskets are wonderful for storing throws and pillows and keeping them accessible. The baskets look nice tucked under a large piece of furniture, such as a hall table.

"There is healing in old trees. Old streets a glamour hold.
Why may not I, as well as these, Grow lovely growing old?" —*Karle Baker*

Every entrance to Cedar Cottage is dressed to greet visitors. The side porch holds one of numerous small tables and chairs sprinkled around the property.

The Cozy Cedar Cottage

Nestled in a quiet, whispering grove of pine trees, sits Cedar Cottage—home of artist Jackie Mathews. The quaint house radiates a peaceful aura that embraces everyone who visits. Guests always comment on how refreshed they feel after a stay.

The vignettes Jackie creates in her home celebrate the simple pleasures in life. Her passion for French style is evident in her choice of fabrics and accessories, and in the décor she creates to greet each season.

(Left) Cedar Cottage is named for the majestic grove of cedar pines that surround it, and for the wooden paneling on most of the walls inside of the house.

"Arranging a bowl of flowers in the morning
can give a sense of quiet in a crowded day
—like writing a poem, or saying a prayer."
—*Anne Morrow Lindbergh*

The bright master bedroom, with its white walls and pine floors, showcases an antique French headboard. A pair of vintage wicker chairs at the foot of the bed makes a delightful spot for reading or conversation.

Orienting a bedroom for the best use of sunlight helps promote calm and well-being. If a room is dark, adding an architectural window close to the ceiling will let in light and maintain privacy.

Quilts scattered throughout the house add color and suggest that comfort is of utmost importance at Cedar Cottage. Quilts can be draped over the backs of chairs, folded neatly in piles under tables, or hung on wall hooks for easy access.

(Left) There is only one option for bathing in this small bathroom—a soak in the tub. Geraniums on the windowsill are hearty and thrive in the sunlight. Flowering plants are wonderful additions to serene spaces.

(Above) A chair placed on top of a table fills an empty corner and holds a collection of favorite books.

(Left) A tea set on a bedside table is a reminder to take time to sit and relax everyday.

113

> "Teach us Delight in simple things,
> And Mirth that has no bitter springs."
> —*Rudyard Kipling*

(Right) A cherished collection of French stationery and writing accessories looks lovely showcased on a writing table. Dried lavender releases a relaxing aromatic scent.

(Below) Clear crystal and cut-glass perfume bottles glisten when displayed on a windowsill.

Serene Secret

A large table may be used as a writing desk. Locate it near a window to take advantage of natural light. Small family photos make the area intimate.

AT HOME IN FRANCE   CHRISTOPHER PETKANAS
Photographs by JEAN-BERNARD NALDIN

HIDDEN TREASURES REVEALED
KOSTENEVICH   ABRADALE

CÉZANNE *by himself*   Kendall

The trend has been to lighten dark wood by painting it white, but sometimes natural wood is much better left alone. What better way to achieve serenity than to enjoy things in their natural state?

"O holy simplicity!"
—*Jan Hess*

(Above) A collection of brass candlestick holders in various sizes is an interesting display on a small table. It's not always necessary to keep precious metals polished. The simpler way to enjoy them is to allow them to develop a tarnished patina.

(Left) Household paperwork can be done at a table and stored in baskets when not being worked on. If a decorative display is kept to a minimum, it can be moved aside when the table is needed for more practical matters.

(Right) The natural brick fireplace blends with the cedar-paneled walls and is the focal point of the sitting room. Baskets hung from the ceiling contribute to the room's cottage ambiance.

(Below) The wooden arms and legs of this wingback chair are painted soft green and accented with gold gilding for an elegant touch.

Using pairs of matching accessories to arrange a mantel display creates balance. Be sure each pair varies in height, shape and color from the other.

Vintage ribbons and lace are a reminder of days when quality and artful workmanship were the norm. They can be a delight to collect and are best enjoyed when kept out on display. Ribbon and lace look lovely arranged in a small basket or in boxes set on a dresser or side table.

Serene Secret

Beautiful ribbons are very decorative, and many times are happy memories of wonderful gifts that came wrapped with them. A vintage doorknob attached to a wall makes a lovely hanging place to display your favorites.

(Right) The table and large mirror in the entry are treasured family antiques and are a gracious welcome for guests. Tall curly willow branches in large vases provide a floral detail without the worry of keeping fresh flowers. Jauntily displayed hats and walking sticks are held in an umbrella stand. Long lengths of ribbon are displayed on a facing wall.

The simple things in life are the best source of serenity. Jackie Matthews features fresh flowers and fruits in vignettes throughout her home. Nature's bounty is always plentiful in her kitchen and is celebrated in the fabrics and needlework on pillows and a footstool.

Fresh fruit and flowers are a natural choice for kitchen displays. Nicely packaged pastas and other nonperishable food items can be stored in a basket under a table so the attractive labels can be enjoyed.

"I go to nature to be soothed and healed, and to have my senses put in order."
—*John Burroughs*

"Very little is needed to make a happy life."
—*Marcus Aurelius Antoninus*

Serene Secrets

• Using favorite kitchen items such as vintage bowls, pitchers and platters to hold flowers and fruit, makes an attractive vignette on a kitchen table.
• A small footstool can be used to elevate objects and make the display more interesting.

The décor of a home doesn't have to be minimalist to be serene. Many people are happiest when surrounded by numerous treasured accessories. Enjoying a collection that has been a pleasure to assemble is just as calming, and can make a home very tranquil and peaceful.

A cottage kitchen can be efficient despite being small. It's easy to air-dry pots and pans by hanging them from a rack. A farmhouse sink gives the kitchen work area charm.

(Left) The paper that Jackie Matthews uses for her watercolor paintings is handmade from materials gathered around the grounds of Cedar Cottage. The paintings are matted on French fabrics, and set in vintage frames, making each work unique. Using fabric as matting is an easy way to make your own pictures and photos match your home décor.

(Below) The porch outside the studio at Cedar Cottage is one of numerous outdoor sitting areas. All-weather cushions stay outside, while the pillows and quilt are put away during bad weather.

(Right) Favorite fabrics are kept on the work table in the studio for inspiration. Whether you are an artist, or your work is of a less creative nature, keeping all your tools at hand will make projects much more enjoyable.

"Remember that happiness is a way of travel—not a destination."
—*Roy M. Goodman*

> "Slow down and enjoy life. It's not only the scenery you miss going too fast—you also miss the sense of where you are going and why."
> —*Eddie Cantor*

(Left) Vignettes are delightful and invite passersby to pause and take a few moments to enjoy the beauty of the outdoors.

(Above and right) The side yard can be as much a living space as the inside of the house. A bistro table and chairs is set in a clearing for quiet meals, and a gazebo frames a sitting area. The furniture stays out year round, while the linens and pillows are taken in when not in use.

Comfortable cushions, quilts or blankets and decorative pillows will make outdoor areas inviting. Choose fabrics that are durable and will look attractive even if they fade in the sunlight. It's a little extra work to bring them in and out of doors, but well worth the effort.

(Right) A gravel walkway creates a natural entrance to an outdoor sitting room. Plants are used to create natural walls on three sides of the area.

(Below) A weathered farmhouse bench is perfect for an outdoor garden display. Balance works just as well with outdoor décor as it does indoors, and is created here by using two urns, two potted trees and two watering cans.

Bare Is Better

With the trend toward painted white wood in cottages, many people might be tempted to paint over natural wood paneling. Consider leaving it in its original state and using a complementary palette of fabrics and accessories to highlight the wood's beauty.

Framed Up

Different sizes of vintage frames make an interesting display when organized on a wall shelf. Newer frames can be coated with antique gold paint for an aged look.

The Cozy Cedar Cottage

Easily Contained

Keep favorite writing accessories in a vintage mail basket. They will stay organized and can be easily moved when you need more workspace.

Paper Pleasures

Stationery from favorite hotels is a delightful souvenir of memorable travels. It's easy to carry home and is an inexpensive keepsake rich with happy memories.

Seasonal Changes for

"The only calendar I need is just outside my window. With eyes to see and ears to hear, nature keeps me posted."
—*Alfred A. Montapert*

Faux finishes on walls add color dimension that will catch and reflect seasonal light changes as the days lengthen and shorten. Often, a wash or other treatment can be applied over existing wall color.

(Above) An outdoor vignette, easily seen from a door or window, is a wonderful way to mark the time of year.

(Right) Chairs are slipcovered in off-white for spring and summer. The covers are easily removed to reveal a vibrant check pattern for fall and winter.

Year-Round Serenity

Artist Tracy Voornas celebrates the arrival and passage of the seasons with simple changes to her décor that puts her home in serene syncronicity with nature. Fabrics are coordinated so pillows and cushions are turned to one color scheme for spring and summer, and another for fall and winter. Her ideas are inspiring for any home.

Make a ritual of the day you make the change, and you'll find that rather than lamenting the passage of time—you are looking forward with hope and joy.

The pillows and cushions on the sofa in the living room are turned twice a year. The neutral fabric on the sofa frame acts as a backdrop for both seasonal color schemes.

A simple change of accessories, such as silk flowers and candles, makes the annual switch easy and fun.

"Every season brings its own joy."
—*Spanish Proverb*

When creating seasonal home décor, choose five or six coordinating fabrics. Design pillows in geometric blocks, and rotate the different fabrics within the design. The fabric that was the primary choice for one seasonal theme can become a coordinate for the other.

A reversible duvet cover on the bed is off-white for summer and the winter side has a floral border on a muted-color fabric. The same pillows are used for both schemes and are turned to reveal different fabrics.

(Above right) The fabric colors on the chaise cushions are light on one side for warmer months, and darker on the other for a cozy feel in fall and winter.

(Above left) Tab-top window valances are reversible and slide off the rod for an easy switch. The tabs hang long for a decorative touch on the spring/summer side.

Simple Serenity in Small-Space Living

"If I ever go searching for my heart's desire again, I'll
never go any further than my own backyard.
Because if it isn't there, I never lost it to begin with."
—Dorothy (in The Wizard of Oz)

Judith Laramore had the courage to follow her passion
when she left a career as a nurse and took up shopkeeping. The
change meant that she would be living in a small space above her
store. It also meant she could live among the things she loves—
vintage and antique collectibles. Because space in her home is at
a premium, she displays her treasured possessions and uses
them regularly.

(Left) If you are a flea market aficionado,
be on the lookout for monograms that
match yours or those of friends. A
friend spotted this vintage nightshirt
and knew it would be appreciated
because of the initials.

(Right) The bed is dressed in a simple
symphony of red and white. Pillowcases
don't have to be vintage to have the
look. These were a lovingly cross-
stitched gift. A reading light hung from
the frame of the bed makes nighttime
reading comfortable.

Attractive stationery and writing accessories are a lovely complement to home décor. Remove note cards and other decorative writing papers from boxes and display them tied with pretty ribbons or trims.

The art of letter writing is one of the greatest ways to pursue serenity. Sitting quietly and editing our thoughts in preparation of conveying them to another is great food for the soul. Even the smallest home should have a special place dedicated to this purpose.

An inviting letter-writing spot does not have to be a desk. A table or piece of comfortable vintage furniture can work just as well.

Invite treasured family members into your serene spaces by displaying their portrait. There is only one rule for decorating a writing area—it needs to bring you comfort and joy to spend time there.

(Above) Vintage threads and their wooden spools make a delightful display when kept in a glass-sided box.

(Right) An antique store counter, used as a kitchen island, is a delightful place to display small treasures. Among the items kept under the glass top are shells collected at the beach, purchases from a Paris flea market and beloved keepsakes from childhood.

"Take a music bath once or twice a week for a few seasons, and you will find that it is to the soul what the water-bath is to the body."
—*William Shakespeare*

Music is an important part of any serene home. Whether it's coming from a beloved piano or a sound system, music relaxes the spirit and helps promote calm and relaxation.

This Victorian piano is surrounded by vintage treasures and is made an important priority in this small living space.

Acknowledgements

Heartfelt thanks to the home owners featured in this book:

The Friendly Farmhouse
Nancy & Gary Bagnall
Arroyo Grande, California

A Mountaintop Manor
Kimberly & John Stanier
San Luis Obispo, California

A Stately Grand Dame
Ann Fraser
Design Services Available Through:
Fraser House & Cie
522 Aliso Avenue
Newport Beach, CA 92663
(949) 646-1778
Email: FraserHous@aol.com

A Bungalow by the Beach
Judy Watkins
Old Edna Says, Well…La de Da!
1653 Old Price Canyon Road
San Luis Obispo, CA 93401
(805) 544-8062
Email: Ladedajudy@charter.net
www.ladedaonline.com

Seasonal Changes
Tracy Voornas
House Calls

Small-Space Living
Judith Laramore and Bonnie Frank
Birds of a Feather
2020 Main Street
Cambria, CA 93428
(805) 927-2391

The Cozy Cedar Cottage
Jackie Matthews
Cambria, California
Jackie's artwork is available
through Birds of a Feather
(805) 927-2391

Index

Serenity, regularity,
absence of vanity,
sincerity, simplicity,
veracity, equanimity,
fixity, non-irritability,
adaptability, humility,
tenacity, integrity,
nobility, magnanimity,
charity, generosity,
purity. Practice daily
these eighteen "ities."
You will soon
attain immortality"
—*Socrates*